The Doll's House and Other Stories

KATHERINE MANSFIELD

Level 4

Retold by Ann Ward
Series Editors: Andy Hopkins and Jocelyn Potter

Pearson Education Limited
Edinburgh Gate, Harlow,
Essex CM20 2JE, England
and Associated Companies throughout the world.

ISBN: 978-1-4058-8213-2

Bliss and *Mr Reginald Peacock's Day* were first published in 1920.
The Doll's House was also first published in 1920 as *Prelude*.
The Garden Party was first published in 1922.
This adaptation first published by Penguin Books 1991
Published by Addison Wesley Longman Ltd and Penguin Books Ltd 1998
New edition first published 1999
This edition first published 2008

3 5 7 9 10 8 6 4 2

Typeset by Graphicraft Ltd, Hong Kong
Set in 11/14pt Bembo
Printed in China
SWTC/02

Published by Pearson Education Ltd in association with
Penguin Books Ltd, both companies being subsidiaries of Pearson Plc

For a complete list of the titles available in the Penguin Readers series please write to your local
Pearson Longman office or to: Penguin Readers Marketing Department, Pearson Education,
Edinburgh Gate, Harlow, Essex CM20 2JE, England.

Contents

Introduction

Playtime came and the girls surrounded Isabel. The girls in her class nearly fought to put their arms around her. The only two outside the group were the little Kelveys. But they were always on the outside.

'The Doll's House' (February 1922) describes a simple event: a doll's house is given to the three Burnell girls as a gift. This 'simple' event, though, shows up the social order of their world. We also see how childish behaviour can continue into adult life.

'Bliss' (August 1918) takes place in London in the safe world of Bertha Young. She is married to Harry and they have a baby daughter. Bertha has nothing to worry about in her life – she has a happy family, servants, a beautiful home and plenty of money. There is a beautiful silvery pear tree in the garden. She feels blissfully happy. Can anything go wrong?

'Mr Reginald Peacock's Day' (June 1917) begins with his wife waking him up with quiet words and a cup of tea. She tries to make him feel guilty by making his breakfast. She argues with him at breakfast. It is war! Or that's what Reginald thinks. But perhaps there is another point of view.

'The Garden Party' (February 1922) shows a young woman called Laura learning the social rules of her class. What happens when a party in her world is affected by events in a neighbouring street of poor houses? She isn't sure that she agrees with the rules but will she fight against them? This story takes place in New Zealand.

Katherine Mansfield was born in Wellington, New Zealand,

in 1888. She was the third of six children – five girls and one boy, although one of the girls died. They were all interested in painting and music. They read books and discussed their ideas. Katherine travelled to England with her family when she was fifteen, and went to school in London for three years. She wrote for the school magazine, began writing a book and learnt to love the work of Oscar Wilde.

After two years back in New Zealand, she missed her London life. 'London – it is Life,' she wrote. She told her father that she must return to England to become a writer. She moved to London when she was twenty, and her father gave her a little money to live on.

She was always changing her look at this time, and wore all kinds of strange clothes. She dressed like a Maori, like a boy, or in Japanese clothes with white make-up.

She fell in love with a musician from New Zealand, but that relationship ended. She married her singing teacher, G. C. Bowden. She came to the wedding in a black suit and shiny black hat, which was very unusual in 1909, and she left him the next day. The character of Reginald Peacock in the second story in this collection is similar to Bowden. She then joined Trowell, who was on tour in Europe with a music company, and soon found she was expecting a baby. Her mother immediately took her to Bavaria in Germany, away from Trowell, but Katherine lost the baby.

In 1911 her first book came out. It was a collection of stories called *In a German Pension*. She then met John Middleton Murry, who was a journalist and ran a magazine called *Rhythm*. They became lovers and stayed together, on and off, for the rest of her life. In 1913 they moved to Paris, but Murry had financial problems, and they returned to London. When the First World War broke out in 1914, Murry tried to join the army. He was refused for health reasons.

In 1915, Mansfield became ill. Her brother Leslie came to London to join the army and was killed in the same year in a training accident in France. Katherine was very upset by the death of her brother, but worked hard and wrote many stories.

She met the leading writers of her day, including D. H. Lawrence, Virginia Woolf and T. S. Eliot. She was very good company and made everyone laugh with her sharp conversation. In 1918, she and Murry finally married.

She travelled between Europe and England a lot during her life, unable to spend the winter months in England because of her health. Sometimes Murry went with her to France or Switzerland; at other times she travelled alone or with a friend. She needed a warm climate to stop her cough, but had very little money to support herself. Away from her husband and her family in New Zealand, she wrote some of her bitterest stories. She died at Fontainebleau in France in 1923. She was only thirty-four.

Two more collections of short stories came out in her lifetime: *Bliss and Other Stories* (1920) and *The Garden Party and Other Stories* (1922). Single stories appeared in magazines, and more collections came out after her death, including *The Dove's Nest and Other Stories* and *Something Childish and Other Stories*. Her husband Murry also produced books of her poems, letters and notebooks.

Katherine Mansfield was part of a very clever group of writers. English literature was pulled into the new century by this group, which included Lawrence, Elliot, Woolf and James Joyce. London was the centre of the literary world at that time.

But Mansfield was still a New Zealander. She drew on childhood experiences in her writing, taking characters, places and events from her home country. She was brought up in Wellington in New Zealand, which is as far away from London as you can get. At that time New Zealand belonged to Britain, and it modelled itself on British middle class life. White New Zealanders then talked of Britain as 'home', even if they had never been there.

Mansfield's stories usually turn on a single moment or sudden event that completely changes a character's life. In 'Bliss' it is the moment when Bertha sees Harry in the hall after the dinner party. In 'The Doll's House' a child behaves badly, mirroring an adult's bad behaviour. This shows us exactly what their society is built on. And in 'The Garden Party' a piece of news from the baker's man pulls a young girl out of her safe world into a meeting with death.

This way of writing was very new at the time. The short story until then had a beginning, a middle, and an end, and one event followed another. Now it was a moment, like a painting by Cézanne or Van Gogh. Or a different way of looking at something, like a painting by Picasso.

The first line of Mansfield's stories often throws us right into the action. The first line of 'Reginald Peacock', for example – 'He hated the way his wife woke him up in the morning.' – tells us several things: the man is married, he finds his wife annoying, he is too stupid to solve his problem by getting himself out of bed, he is too lazy to get up first. We read Mansfield's first line and immediately start to build the story in our minds. A short story writer only has our attention for a short time, so the story needs to get going quickly. A short story is like listening to a conversation – we have to add the missing information. Mansfield does not tell us how old any of her characters are, for example – she does not have time – but we may guess that Kezia is about eleven and Laura is about seventeen.

Her simple subject matter – such as the arrival of a doll's house, the giving of a dinner party – leads to a sharp criticism of the social order. She does not write about big historical or political events, and yet she makes us think just as effectively about society and political ideas.

The stories ask more questions than they answer. In Reginald Peacock's story, for example, she is asking 'What kind of man is this? Should men rule society if they are like this?' She leaves her readers to think about it.

We have to give meaning to the small details that stay in our minds after we read. What does the lamp in 'The Doll's House' mean, for example? Is it the light that the whole story throws on the world, is it the strong light that burns in young Kezia, who does not accept rules without question? Does the pear tree in 'Bliss' make us think of the silvery Miss Fulton? It stands at the heart of Bertha's garden. Does Miss Fulton stand at the heart of Bertha's world?

Mansfield's main characters are often children. Their innocent way of looking can open up the adult world. Some of the characters we meet in this collection, such as the Burnells and the Sheridans, also appear in other stories. The child Kezia and teenager Laura question ideas, attitudes and ways of behaving. Kezia leaves safe places to find out about the unknown, as Laura does when she goes down to the Scotts' world.

Mansfield's stories can be worrying for her readers. She takes them into an ordinary world and shows them a normal life. She describes its colours, light, flowers, nature, a life they can easily imagine. But there is always a nervous edge to the story. Readers know that something unexpected is going to happen and they wait for it as they read.

Although the world of Katherine Mansfield's time has largely disappeared, we still recognise her sharp and funny pictures of human behaviour. Some things never change.

Bliss

Although Bertha Young was thirty, she still sometimes wanted to run instead of walk. She wanted to dance in the street. She wanted to throw something up in the air and catch it again, or to stand still and laugh at – nothing – at nothing, simply.

What can you do if you are thirty and, suddenly, turning the corner of your own street, you feel perfectly happy, as if you had swallowed a piece of the late afternoon sun?

She ran up the steps of her house and felt in her bag for her key, but she had forgotten it, as usual. The servant opened the door.

'Thank you, Mary,' she said as she went in. 'Is Nurse back?'

'Yes, Ma'am.'

'And has the fruit come?'

'Yes, Ma'am. Everything's come.'

'Bring the fruit into the dining-room, will you? I'll arrange it before I go upstairs.'

It was quite dark and cold in the dining-room. But Bertha still threw off her coat, and the cold air fell on her arms.

But she still had that feeling of perfect happiness, as if she had swallowed a piece of sunshine. She did not want to breathe. The feeling might get stronger; but still she breathed, deeply, deeply. She did not want to look in the cold mirror, but still she did look, and saw a woman with smiling lips and big, dark eyes. She looked as if she was waiting for somebody, as if she was waiting for something to happen. Something must happen.

Mary brought the fruit and with it a glass bowl and a lovely blue dish.

'Shall I turn on the light, Ma'am?'

'No, thank you. I can see quite well.'

There were small oranges and pink apples. There were some smooth yellow pears and some silvery white grapes, and a big bunch of purple grapes. She had bought the purple ones because they matched the colour of the dining-room carpet. Yes, that was silly, but that was why she had bought them. She had thought in the shop: 'I must have some purple ones because of the carpet.'

When she had finished arranging the bright fruit, she stood away from the table to look at them. The glass dish and the blue bowl seemed to hang in the air above the dark table. This was so beautiful that she started to laugh.

'No. No. I mustn't.' And she ran upstairs to her child's room.

♦

Nurse sat at a low table giving little B her supper after her bath. The baby looked up when she saw her mother and began to jump.

'Now, my love, eat it up like a good girl,' said Nurse.

Bertha knew that Nurse did not like her to come in at the wrong time.

'Has she been good, Nurse?'

'She's been a little sweet all afternoon,' whispered Nurse. 'We went to the park and a big dog came along. She pulled its ear. Oh, you should have seen her.'

Bertha wanted to say that it was dangerous to pull a strange dog's ear, but she was rather afraid of Nurse. She stood watching them, her hands by her side, like the poor little girl in front of the rich little girl.

The baby looked up at her again, and then smiled so charmingly that Bertha cried: 'Oh, Nurse, please let me finish giving her supper while you put the bath things away.'

'Well, Ma'am, we oughtn't to change her over while she's eating,' said Nurse.

How silly it was. Why have a baby if it always has to be in another woman's arms?

'Oh I must!' she said.

Nurse was not pleased, but she gave her the baby.

'Now don't excite her after supper.'

Nurse went out of the room with the bath towels.

'Now I've got you to myself, my little jewel,' said Bertha.

When the soup was finished, Bertha turned round to the fire.

'You're nice – you're very nice!' she said, kissing her warm baby. Again, she felt perfectly happy.

'You're wanted on the telephone,' said Nurse, as she took the baby from Bertha. Nurse looked pleased.

♦

She ran downstairs and picked up the telephone. It was Harry.

'Oh, is that you, Ber? Look here. I'll be late. I'll take a taxi and come along as quickly as I can, but can we have dinner ten minutes later? All right?'

'Yes, perfectly all right. Oh, Harry!'

'Yes?'

What did she want to say? She had nothing to say. She only wanted to tell him what she was feeling. It would be silly to say: 'Hasn't it been a wonderful day?'

'What is it?' asked the voice on the telephone.

'Nothing,' said Bertha.

♦

There were people coming to dinner. Mr and Mrs Norman Knight were an interesting couple. He was going to start a theatre, and she was interested in furniture. There was a young man, Eddie Warren, who had just written a little book of poems. Everybody was asking Eddie Warren to dinner. And there was a 'find' of Bertha's, a young woman called Pearl Fulton. Bertha did not know what Miss Fulton did. They had met at the club and Bertha liked her immediately. She always liked beautiful women who had something strange about them.

Bertha and Miss Fulton had met a number of times, and they had talked together a lot, but Bertha still could not understand her friend. Miss Fulton told Bertha everything about some parts of her life, but beyond that she told her nothing.

Was there anything beyond it? Harry said 'No'. He thought Miss Fulton was boring, and 'cold, like all fair-haired women, and perhaps not very intelligent'. But Bertha did not agree with him.

'No, the way she has of sitting with her head a little on one side, and smiling, has something behind it, Harry, and I must find out what it is.'

'Most likely it's a good stomach,' answered Harry.

She went into the sitting-room and lighted the fire and rearranged the furniture a little. The room came alive at once.

The windows of the sitting-room opened onto the garden. At the far end of the garden, against the wall, there was a tall pear tree in full flower. It stood perfect against the light green sky. A grey cat moved slowly across the grass, and a black cat followed it like a shadow. Bertha had a strange, cold feeling when she saw them.

'How strange cats are!' she said, and she turned away from the window and began walking up and down . . .

The smell of flowers filled the warm room. She sat down and pressed her hands to her eyes.

'I'm too happy – too happy!' she said to herself. Really – really – she had everything. She was young. Harry and she were as

At the far end of the garden, against the wall, there was a tall pear tree in full flower.

much in love as ever, and they were really good friends. She had a lovely baby. They didn't have to worry about money. They had a wonderful house and garden. And friends – modern, exciting friends, writers and painters and people who wrote poems – just the kind of friends they wanted.

She sat up. She felt weak with happiness. It must be the spring.

♦

She wore a white dress, a string of green stones around her neck, green shoes and stockings. She looked like the pear tree, but this was accidental. She had decided what to wear before she looked through the sitting-room window.

She kissed Mrs Norman Knight,★ who was wearing an unusual orange coat with a row of black monkeys around the edge.

'Everybody on the train looked at my monkeys!' said Mrs Norman Knight. 'They didn't even laugh. Just looked.'

'And then,' said her husband, 'she turned to the woman beside her and said: "Haven't you ever seen a monkey before?"'

'Oh, yes!' Mrs Norman Knight joined in the laughter. 'Wasn't that just too funny!'

And a funnier thing still was, that now with her coat off, Mrs Norman Knight looked just like an intelligent monkey. Her yellow dress looked like banana skins.

The bell rang. It was Eddie Warren, white-faced and thin. As usual, he looked terribly worried.

'It *is* the right house, *isn't it?*' he asked.

'Oh, I think so – I hope so,' said Bertha brightly.

'I have had such a *terrible* time with a taxi driver; he was *most* strange. I couldn't get him to *stop*. The *more* I tried, the *faster* he went.'

★ Married women used to sometimes be called by their husband's first name in English. This does not often happen now.

He took off his coat. Bertha noticed that his socks were white, too – most charming and unusual.

'But how terrible!' she cried.

'Yes, it really was,' said Eddie, following her into the sitting-room. He knew the Norman Knights. In fact, he was going to write something for Norman Knight when the theatre opened.

'Well, Warren, how's the writing?' said Norman Knight.

And Mrs Norman Knight said: 'Oh, Mr Warren, what happy socks!'

'I *am* so glad you like them,' he said, looking down at his feet. 'They seem to look so *much* whiter when there is a moon.' And he turned his thin sad face to Bertha. There *is* a moon, you know.'

He really was a most attractive person. And so were the Norman Knights.

The front door opened and shut. Harry shouted: 'Hello, you people. Down in five minutes.' They heard him hurry up the stairs. Bertha smiled, she knew how Harry liked to be always busy.

She liked his enthusiasm and his love of fighting. To other people he sometimes seemed strange, but they did not know him well. She understood him. She talked and laughed until Harry came down. She had forgotten that Pearl Fulton had not arrived.

'I wonder if Miss Fulton has forgotten?'

'Probably,' said Harry. 'Is she on the phone?'

'Ah! There's a taxi now.' And Bertha smiled when she thought about her new friend. 'She lives in taxis.'

'She'll get fat if she does,' said Harry coolly, ringing the bell for dinner.

'Harry – don't,' warned Bertha, laughing at him.

They waited, and then Miss Fulton came in. She was all in silver, and she smiled with her head a little on one side.

'Am I late?'

She took Miss Fulton's arm and they moved into the dining-room.

'No, not at all,' said Bertha. 'Come along.' And she took Miss Fulton's arm and they moved into the dining-room. The touch of that cool arm gave Bertha that same perfectly happy feeling again.

Miss Fulton did not look at her, but then she rarely looked straight at people. Her heavy eyelids lay upon her eyes and the strange half-smile came and went on her lips. She seemed to live by listening more than by seeing. But Bertha felt as if they were very close, as if they understood each other very well.

She and Miss Fulton were closer, Bertha felt, than the other guests, as they all ate dinner and talked together. They were all dears, and she loved having them there at her table. She loved giving them wonderful food and wine. In fact, she wanted to tell them how delightful they were, how nice they looked.

Harry was enjoying his dinner. He enjoyed talking about food. Bertha was pleased when he turned to her and said: 'Bertha, this is wonderful!'

She felt as if she loved the whole world. Everything was good – was right.

And still, in the back of her mind, there was the pear tree. It would be silver now, in the light of poor dear Eddie's moon, as silver as Miss Fulton.

It was wonderful how Bertha seemed to understand immediately how Miss Fulton was feeling. She was sure that she understood her new friend perfectly.

'I believe that this does happen sometimes. It happens very, very rarely between women. Never between men,' thought Bertha. 'Perhaps while I am making the coffee in the sitting-room, she will give a sign to show me that she understands, too.'

While she thought like this she continued talking and laughing. She could not stop laughing.

♦

At last, the meal was over.

'Come and see my new coffee machine,' said Bertha.

Mrs Norman Knight sat beside the fire. She was always cold.

At that moment, Miss Fulton 'gave the sign'.

'Do you have a garden?' said the cool, sleepy voice.

Bertha crossed the room, pulled the curtains back, and opened those long windows.

'There!' she breathed.

And the two women stood side by side, looking at the flowering tree. It seemed to grow taller and taller in the bright air. It seemed almost to touch the edge of the round, silver moon.

How long did they stand there? They understood each other perfectly. They were in a circle of light; they were like people from another world.

Then the coffee was ready and Harry said: 'My dear Mrs Knight, don't ask me about my baby. I never see her.'

They talked about Norman Knight's theatre. Mrs Knight talked about the furniture that she was choosing for some people. They talked about a terrible poem about a girl in a wood...

Miss Fulton sat in the lowest, deepest chair and Harry offered cigarettes.

From the way he offered Miss Fulton the cigarette box, Bertha could see that Miss Fulton not only bored Harry; he really disliked her. And she decided that Miss Fulton felt this too, and was hurt.

'Oh, Harry, don't dislike her,' Bertha said to herself. 'You are quite wrong about her. She's wonderful. And besides, how can you feel so differently about someone who means so much to me? I shall try to tell you all about it when we are in bed tonight.'

♦

At those last words, Bertha suddenly thought: 'Soon these people will go. The house will be quiet. The lights will be out. And you and he will be alone together.'

She jumped up from her chair and ran over to the piano.

'What a pity someone does not play!' she cried.

For the first time in her life, Bertha Young wanted her husband.

Oh, she had been in love with him, of course. But her feelings were different from his. They talked together about it – they were such good friends.

But now she felt different. She really wanted him. Was this the meaning of that feeling of perfect happiness?

'My dear,' said Mrs Norman Knight to Bertha, 'we mustn't miss our train. It's been so nice.'

'I'll come with you to the door,' said Bertha. 'I loved having you.'

'Good-night, goodbye,' she cried from the top step.

When she got back into the sitting-room the others were getting ready to leave.

'. . . Then you can come part of the way in my taxi.'

'I shall be *so* thankful *not* to have to take *another* taxi *alone* after the *terrible* time I had before.'

'You can get a taxi at the end of the street. It isn't far to walk.'

'That's good. I'll go and put on my coat.'

Miss Fulton moved towards the door and Bertha was following when Harry almost pushed past.

'Let me help you.'

Bertha knew that Harry was feeling sorry for his rudeness to Miss Fulton, so she let him go. He was like a little boy in some ways, so simple.

Eddie and she stood by the fire.

'Have you seen Bilks' *new* poem about *soup?*' said Eddie softly. 'It's *so* wonderful. Have you got a copy of his new book? I'd *so*

His lips said, 'I love you,' and Miss Fulton laid her white fingers on his cheek and smiled her sleepy smile.

like to *show* it to you. The first line is wonderful: "Why must it always be tomato soup?" '

'Yes,' said Bertha. And she moved silently to a table opposite the sitting-room door and Eddie went silently after her. She picked up the little book and gave it to him; they had not made a sound.

While he looked for the poem in the book she turned her head towards the hall. And she saw... Harry with Miss Fulton's coat in his arms and Miss Fulton with her back turned to him and her head bent. Harry threw the coat down, put his hands on her shoulders and turned her to him. His lips said: 'I love you,' and Miss Fulton laid her white fingers on her cheeks and smiled her sleepy smile. Harry smiled too, and he whispered: 'Tomorrow,' and with her eyelids Miss Fulton said: 'Yes.'

'Here it is,' said Eddie. ' "Why must it always be tomato soup?" It's so *deeply* true, don't you feel? It always *is* tomato soup.'

'If you prefer,' said Harry's voice, very loud, from outside, 'I can phone for a taxi.'

'Oh, no. It's not necessary,' said Miss Fulton, and she came up to Bertha and gave her the thin white fingers to hold.

'Goodbye. Thank you so much.'

'Goodbye,' said Bertha.

Miss Fulton held her hand a moment longer.

'Your lovely pear tree!' she said in a low voice.

And then she was gone, with Eddie following, like the black cat following the grey cat.

'I'll lock the doors,' said Harry, very calmly.

'Your lovely pear tree – pear tree – pear tree!'

Bertha ran to the long windows.

'Oh, what is going to happen now?' she cried.

But the pear tree was as lovely as ever and as full of flowers and as still.

Mr Reginald Peacock's Day

He hated the way his wife woke him up in the morning. She did it on purpose, of course. It showed that she was angry with him. But he was not going to show her that he was angry. But it was really dangerous to wake up an artist like that! It made him feel bad for hours – simply hours.

She came into the room in her working clothes, with a handkerchief over her head, just to show him that she had been awake and working for hours. She called in a low warning voice: 'Reginald!'

'Eh! What! What's that? What's the matter?'

'It's time to get up. It's half-past eight.' And then she left the room, shutting the door quietly behind her. He supposed that she felt very pleased with herself.

He turned over in the big bed. His heart felt heavy. She seemed to enjoy making life more difficult for him; more difficult than it was already. She made an artist's life impossible. She wanted to pull him down, to make him like herself.

What was the matter with her? What did she want? Didn't he have three times as many pupils now as he did when they were first married? Didn't he earn three times as much money? Hadn't he paid for everything they owned? He now had begun to pay for Adrian's school, too. She didn't have any money, but he never said that to her. Never!

When you married a woman she wanted everything. Nothing was worse for an artist than marriage. Artists should wait until they are over forty before they get married. Why had he married her? He asked himself this question about three times a day, but he never could answer it. She had caught him at a weak moment.

Looking back, he saw himself as a poor young thing, half-child, half-wild bird. He was totally unable to manage bills and things like that. Well, she had tried hard to change him, and she was changing him with her early morning trick. An artist ought to wake slowly, he thought, moving down in the warm bed. He began to imagine delightful pictures, one after the other. The pictures ended with his latest, most charming pupil putting her arms around him and covering him with her long hair. 'Awake, my love! . . .'

As usual, while the bath water ran, Reginald Peacock tried his voice.

'*When her mother sees her before the laughing mirror, Tying up her shoes and tying up her hair.*'

He sang softly at first, listening to the quality of his voice, until he came to the third line:

'*Often she thinks, were this wild thing married . . .*' and when he got to the last word his voice became a shout, and a glass on the bathroom shelf shook . . .

Well, there was nothing wrong with his voice, he thought, as he jumped into the bath and covered his soft pink body with soap. He could fill a very large theatre with that voice! He sang again as he took the towel and dried himself quickly.

He returned to his bedroom and began to do his exercises – deep breathing, bending forward and back. He was terribly afraid of getting fat. Men in his job often did get fat. However, there was no sign of fatness at present. He was, he decided, just right. In fact, he felt deeply satisfied when he looked at himself in the mirror, dressed in a black coat, dark grey trousers, grey socks and a black and silver tie. He was not vain, of course – he hated vain men – no, the feeling he had when he looked at himself was purely artistic.

People often asked him if he was really English. They could never believe that he didn't have some Southern blood.

His singing had an emotional quality that was not English . . .

The door began to open and Adrian's head appeared.

'Please, Father, Mother says breakfast is ready, please.'

'Very well,' said Reginald. Then just as Adrian disappeared: 'Adrian!'

'Yes, father.'

'You haven't said "Good morning".'

A few months ago, Reginald had spent a weekend with a very important family, where the father received his little sons in the morning and shook hands with them. Reginald thought that this was charming. He immediately started to do the same in his own home, but Adrian felt silly when he had to shake hands with his own father every morning. And why did his father always sound like he was singing to him instead of talking?

Reginald walked into the dining-room and sat down. There was a pile of letters, a copy of the newspaper and a little covered dish in front of him. He looked quickly at the letters and then at his breakfast. There were two thin pieces of bacon and one egg.

'Don't you want any bacon?' he asked.

'No, I prefer an apple. I don't need bacon every morning.'

Now, what did she mean? Did she mean that she didn't want to cook bacon for him every morning?

'If you don't want to cook the breakfast,' he said, 'why don't you have a servant? We have enough money, and you know how I hate to see my wife doing the work. I know that all the servants we had in the past were mistakes. They stopped my practising and I couldn't have any pupils in the house. But now, you have stopped trying to find the right kind of servant. You could teach a servant, couldn't you?'

'But I prefer to do the work myself; it makes life so much more peaceful . . . Run along, Adrian dear, and get ready for school.'

'Oh, no, that's not it!' Reginald pretended to smile. 'You do

'You do the work yourself, because you want me to feel bad.' Reginald felt pleased with himself and opened an envelope.

the work yourself, because, I don't know why, you want me to feel bad. You may not realize this, but it's true.' He felt pleased with himself and opened an envelope...

Dear Mr Peacock,

I feel that I cannot go to sleep until I have thanked you for the wonderful pleasure your singing gave me this evening. It was quite unforgettable. It made me wonder if the ordinary world is everything there is. Some of us can perhaps understand that there is more in the world, more beauty and richness to enjoy. The house is so quiet. I wish you were here now. Then I could thank you again face to face. You are doing a great thing. You are teaching the world to escape from life!

Yours, most sincerely,
Aenone Fell

PS I am in every afternoon this week...

He felt proud. 'Oh well, don't let us argue about it,' he said, and actually held out his hand to his wife.

But she was not generous enough to answer him.

'I must hurry and take Adrian to school,' she said. 'Your room is ready for you.'

Very well – very well – it was war between them! Well, he would not be the first to make it up again!

He walked up and down his room. He was not calm again until he heard the front door close as Adrian and his wife left. Of course, if this went on, he would have to make some other arrangement. That was obvious.

How could he help the world to escape from life? He opened the piano and checked the list of pupils for the morning. Miss Betty Brittle, the Countess Wilkowska and Miss Marian Morrow. They were charming, all three.

At half-past ten exactly, the doorbell rang. He went to the door. Miss Betty Brittle was there, dressed in white with her music in a blue case.

'I'm afraid I'm early,' she said shyly, and she opened her big blue eyes very wide. 'Am I?'

'Not at all, dear lady. I am only too charmed,' said Reginald, 'Won't you come in?'

'It's such a beautiful morning,' said Miss Brittle, 'I walked across the park. The flowers were wonderful.'

'Well, think about the flowers while you sing your exercises,' said Reginald, sitting down at the piano. 'It will give your voice colour and warmth.'

'Oh, what a charming idea! How clever Mr Peacock is!' Miss Brittle thought. She opened her pretty lips and began to sing like a flower.

'Very good, very good!' said Reginald, as he played the piano.

'Make the notes round. Don't be afraid. Breathe the music.'

How pretty she looked, standing there in her white dress, her little fair head raised, showing her milky neck.

'Do you ever practise in front of a mirror?' asked Reginald. 'You ought to, you know. Come over here.'

They went across the room to the mirror and stood side by side. 'Now sing – moo-e-koo-e-oo-e-a!'

But she could not sing, and her face became pinker than ever.

'Oh,' she cried, 'I can't. It makes me feel so silly. It makes me want to laugh. I look so silly!'

'No, you don't. Don't be afraid,' said Reginald, but he laughed, too, very kindly. 'Now, try again!'

The lesson went past very quickly, and Betty Brittle stopped feeling shy.

'When can I come again?' she asked, tying the music up in the blue case. 'I want to take as many lessons as I can just now. Oh, Mr Peacock, I *do* enjoy them so much. May I come the day after tomorrow?'

'Dear lady, I shall be only too charmed,' said Reginald, as he showed her out.

Wonderful girl! And when they had stood in front of the mirror, her white sleeve had just touched his black one. He could feel – yes, he could actually feel a warm place on his sleeve, and he touched it. She loved her lessons.

His wife came in.

'Reginald, can you let me have some money? I must pay for the milk. And will you be in for dinner tonight?'

'Yes, you know I'm singing at Lord Timbuck's at half-past nine. Can you give me some clear soup, with an egg in it?'

'Yes. And the money, Reginald.' She told him how much she needed.

'That's a lot of money – isn't it?'

'No – that's what it should be. And Adrian must have milk.'

There she was again. Now she was talking about Adrian.

'I certainly don't want to stop my child having enough milk,' he said. 'Here's the money.'

The doorbell rang. He went to the door.

'Oh,' said the Countess Wilkowska, 'the stairs. I'm out of breath.' And she put her hand over her heart as she followed him into the music room. She was all in black, with a little black hat and a bunch of fresh flowers on her dress.

'Do not make me sing exercises, today,' she said, throwing out her hands in her delightful foreign way. 'No, today, I want only to sing songs . . . And may I take off my flowers? They die so soon.'

'They die so soon – they die so soon,' played Reginald on the piano.

'May I put them there?' asked the Countess, putting the flowers in front of one of the photographs of Reginald.

'Dear lady, I shall be only too charmed!' said Reginald.

She began to sing, and all went well until she came to the words: 'You love me. Yes, I *know* you love me!' His hands dropped down from the piano, and he turned round, facing her.

'No, no, that's not good enough. You can do better than that!' Reginald cried. 'You must sing as if you were in love. Listen: let me try and show you.' And he sang.

'Oh, yes, yes. I see what you mean,' said the little Countess. 'May I try again?'

'Certainly. Do not be afraid. Let yourself go!' he called above the music. And he sang.

'Yes, better that time. But still I feel that you could do better. Try it with me.' And they sang together.

Ah! Now she was sure she understood. 'May I try once again?'

'You love me. Yes, I *know* you love me.'

'May I put them there?' asked the Countess, putting the flowers in front
of one of the photographs of Reginald.

The lesson was over before those words were quite perfect. Her little foreign hands shook as they put the music together.

'And you are forgetting your flowers,' said Reginald softly.

'Yes, I think I will forget them,' said the Countess, biting her lip.

'And you will come to my house on Sunday and make music?' she asked.

'Dear lady, I shall be only too charmed!' said Reginald.

♦

Miss Marian Morrow arrived . . . She began to sing a sad little song, and her eyes filled with tears.

'Don't sing just now,' said Reginald. 'Let me play it for you.' He played so softly.

'Is there anything the matter?' asked Reginald. 'You're not quite happy this morning.'

No, she wasn't, she was awfully sad.

'Would you tell me what it is?'

It really wasn't anything. Sometimes, she felt that life was very hard.

'Ah, I know,' he said, 'if I could only help!'

'But you do help, you do! Oh, these lessons are so important to me.'

'Sit down in the armchair and smell these flowers and let me sing to you. It will do you as much good as a lesson.'

Why weren't all men like Mr Peacock?

'I wrote a poem after I heard you sing last night – just about what I felt. Of course, it wasn't *personal*. May I send it to you?'

'Dear lady, I would be only too charmed!'

By the end of the afternoon, he was quite tired, and lay down on a sofa to rest his voice before dressing. The door of his room was open. He could hear Adrian and his wife talking in the dining-room.

'Do you know what the teapot reminds me of, Mummy? It reminds me of a little sitting-down cat.'

'Does it, Mr Imagination?'

Reginald slept. The telephone bell woke him.

'Aenone Fell speaking. Mr Peacock, I have just heard that you are singing at Lord Timbuck's tonight. Will you have dinner with me? We can go on together afterwards.'

And the words of his reply dropped like flowers down the telephone.

'Dear lady, I shall be only too charmed.'

♦

What an evening! The little dinner with Aenone Fell, the drive to Lord Timbuck's in her white car, when again she thanked him for the unforgettable pleasure of his singing. And Lord Timbuck's wine!

'Have some more wine, Peacock,' said Lord Timbuck. Lord Timbuck did not call him Mr Peacock, he called him Peacock, as if he were a friend. And wasn't he a friend? He was an artist. Wasn't he teaching them all to escape from life? How he sang! And how they all listened to him!

'Have another glass of wine, Peacock.'

'They all love me. I could have anyone I liked by lifting a finger,' thought Peacock as he walked home with uncertain steps.

But as he let himself into the dark flat the wonderful feeling of happiness began to disappear. He turned on the light in his bedroom. His wife was asleep on her side of the bed. He remembered suddenly the conversation they had had earlier.

'I'm going out to dinner,' he had said.

'But why didn't you tell me before?'

'Must you always talk to me like that? Must you always be so rude?' he had told her. He could not believe that she wasn't interested in all his wonderful artistic successes. So many other

24

'They all love me. I could have anyone I liked by lifting a finger,'
thought Reginald.

women would have been so happy... Yes, he knew it... Why
not say it? And there she was, an enemy, even when she was
sleeping.

Must it always be the same? he thought, the wine still
working. Can't we be friends? If we were friends I could tell her
so much now! About this evening: even about the way Lord
Timbuck talked to me, and all that they said to me and so on and
so on. If only I felt that she were here to come back to – that I
could tell her everything – and so on and so on.

He felt so emotional that he pulled off his evening boot and
threw it in the corner of the room. The noise woke his wife. She
sat up suddenly, pushing back her hair. And he suddenly decided
to try one more time to talk to her like a friend, to tell her

everything, to win her. He sat down on the side of the bed and took one of her hands. But he could not say any of the wonderful things he wanted to say. To his surprise, the only words he could say were: 'Dear lady, I should be so charmed – so charmed!'

The Doll's House

When old Mrs Hay went back to town after staying with the Burnells, she sent the children a doll's house. The doll's house was so big that two men had to carry it. It stood outside the Burnells' house, on two boxes. The doll's house was safe outside; it was summer. It smelled of paint. Perhaps when winter came, and they had to carry it inside, the smell would be gone. Because, really, the smell was awful.

'It was sweet of old Mrs Hay to give the children a present; most sweet and kind,' said the children's Aunt Beryl when they unpacked the doll's house. 'But the smell of paint is enough to make anyone seriously ill.'

The doll's house was green, dark and oily, and bright yellow. There was a door, yellow and shiny, and there were four windows, real windows.

But what a perfect, perfect little house! Who could possibly be worried about the smell? It was part of the feeling of happiness, part of the newness.

'Open it quickly, someone!'

At first, they could not open it, it was too stiff and new, but at last, the whole house front opened. And there you were, staring straight into the rooms, the living-room, the dining-room, the kitchen and the two bedrooms. That is the way for a house to open! Why don't all houses open like that? It was much more exciting than just looking in through a narrow front door!

'Oh-oh!' The girls' cries sounded almost sad. The doll's house was too wonderful; it was too much for the Burnell children. They had never seen anything like it in their lives. There were pictures on the wall. Red carpet covered all the floors except the kitchen. There were red chairs in the living-room and green

The girls looked at the doll's house; and more than anything Kezia liked the lamp.

chairs in the dining-room, there were tables, and beds with real covers, there was a cooker, and shelves with tiny plates and a jug.

But more than anything, Kezia liked the lamp. The lamp stood in the middle of the dining-room table, a little yellow and white lamp.

The father and mother dolls, who sat stiffly in the living-room, and their two little children asleep upstairs, were really too big for the doll's house. They didn't look as if they belonged there. But the lamp was perfect. It seemed to smile at Kezia, to say: 'I live here.' The lamp was real.

♦

The Burnell children could hardly walk fast enough to school the next morning. They wanted to tell everybody, proudly to describe their doll's house before the school bell rang.

'I'll tell them,' said Isabel, 'because I'm the eldest. And you two can join in after. But I'm going to tell first.'

There was nothing to answer. Isabel was always right, and Lottie and Kezia knew this. So they walked along the road to school and said nothing.

'And then I'll choose who's going to come and see it first. Mother said I could bring someone.'

Their mother had told them that they could ask the girls from school to come and look at the doll's house, while it stood outside. The girls could come two at a time. They could not stay for tea, or come into the house, though. But they could stand quietly outside, while Isabel pointed to all the beautiful things in the doll's house, and Lottie and Kezia looked pleased . . .

But even though they hurried to school, the bell was ringing as they arrived at the gate. They didn't have time to tell the others about the doll's house, after all. But Isabel looked very important

Isabel stood under the trees and the little girls pressed up close. The only two who stayed outside the group were the little Kelveys.

and whispered behind her hand to the girls near her, 'Got something to tell you at playtime.'

Playtime came and the girls surrounded Isabel. The girls in her class nearly fought to put their arms around her, to walk away with her, to be her special friend. Isabel stood under the trees and the little girls pressed up close. And the only two who stayed outside the group were the little Kelveys. But they were always on the outside. They knew better than to come anywhere near the Burnells.

The fact was, the school was not really the kind of school that the Burnells wanted their children to go to. But it was the only school for miles. So all the children in the neighbourhood, rich and poor, went there. But the Kelveys were different from all the rest. Many of the parents, including the Burnells, even told their children that they must not speak to the Kelveys. And so the other girls, led by the Burnells, walked past the Kelveys with their noses in the air. Even the teacher had a special voice for the Kelveys, and a special smile for the other children when Lil Kelvey brought her a bunch of sad-looking flowers.

The Kelveys were the daughters of a hard-working little woman who went from house to house washing people's clothes. This was awful enough. But where was Mr Kelvey? Nobody knew for certain. But everybody said he was in prison. Very nice friends for other people's children! And their appearance! People said that they couldn't understand why Mrs Kelvey dressed her children in such strange clothes. The truth was that the people Mrs Kelvey worked for sometimes gave her old things that they did not need. She used these things to dress her children.

Lil Kelvey, the older girl, for instance, came to school in a skirt made from the Burnells' old green tablecover, and a blouse made from the Logans' old red curtains. Her hat used to belong to Miss Lecky, who worked in the post office. Lil really looked very funny – it was impossible not to laugh at her. And her little sister, Else, wore a long white dress and a pair of little boy's boots. But Else looked strange all the time. She was small and thin, with very short hair, and enormous eyes. Nobody had ever seen her smile, and she rarely spoke. She spent her life holding on to Lil, a piece of Lil's skirt held tight in her hand. Where Lil went, Else followed.

Now, they stood on the edge of the group of girls; you couldn't stop them listening. When the little girls turned round and looked at them coldly, Lil, as usual, gave her silly smile, but Else only looked.

And Isabel's voice, very proud, continued telling. The girls were excited when they heard about the carpet, and the beds with real covers, and the cooker with an oven door.

When she had finished, Kezia said, 'You've forgotten the lamp, Isabel.'

'Oh yes,' said Isabel, 'and there's a little lamp, all made of yellow glass, that stands on the dining-room table. It looks just like a real one.'

'The lamp's best of all,' cried Kezia. She thought Isabel wasn't telling the girls enough about the little lamp. But nobody was listening to her, because now Isabel was choosing two girls to come back with them after school and look at the doll's house. She chose Emmie Cole and Lena Logan. But when the others knew that they were all going to have a chance to see the doll's house, they were very, very nice to Isabel. One by one, they put their arms around Isabel's waist and walked away with her. They had something to whisper to her, a secret, 'Isabel's *my* friend.'

Only the little Kelveys moved away, forgotten – there was nothing more for them to hear.

♦

Days passed, and more and more children saw the doll's house. It was all they talked about.

'Have you seen the Burnells' doll's house?'

'Oh, isn't it lovely!'

'Haven't you seen it yet? Oh, dear!'

Even in the lunch hour, they talked about it. The little girls sat under the trees eating their thick meat sandwiches and big pieces of cake. All the time, the Kelveys were sitting as near as they could. They listened too, little Else holding on to Lil, as they ate their jam sandwiches out of a newspaper.

♦

'Mother,' said Kezia, 'can't I ask the Kelveys just once?'

'Certainly not, Kezia.'

'But why not?'

'Run away, Kezia, you know quite well why not.'

♦

At last, everybody had seen the doll's house except the Kelveys. On that day, the little girls were not quite so interested in the subject. It was the lunch hour. The children were standing together under the trees. Suddenly, as they looked at the Kelveys, eating out of their paper, always by themselves, always listening, they wanted to be nasty to them. Emmie Cole started the whisper.

'Lil Kelvey's going to be a servant when she grows up.'

'O-oh, how awful!' said Isabel Burnell, and she looked back at Emmie with very wide eyes.

Emmie swallowed and nodded to Isabel. She had often seen her mother swallow and nod like that at similar times.

'It's true – it's true – it's true,' she said.

Lena Logan looked very interested. 'Shall I ask her?' she whispered.

'You wouldn't,' said Jessie May.

'Pooh, I'm not frightened,' said Lena. Suddenly, she jumped up and danced in front of the other girls. 'Watch! Watch me! Watch me now!' said Lena. And moving slowly along, laughing behind her hand, and looking back at the others, Lena went over to the Kelveys.

Lil looked up from her lunch. She put the rest of her jam sandwich away quickly. Else also stopped eating. What was coming now?

'Is it true you're going to be a servant when you grow up, Lil Kelvey?' Lena cried.

Dead silence. But instead of answering, Lil only gave her silly smile. The question didn't seem to worry her at all. Poor Lena!

Her friends smiled at each other and even began to laugh a little.

Lena got angry. She moved closer to Lil and Else and spoke to them through her teeth. 'Yah, your father's in prison!' she said, quite clearly.

This was such a wonderful thing to say that the little girls all rushed away, deeply, deeply excited, and wild with happiness. Someone found a long rope and they began skipping. And they had never skipped so high, or run in and out of ropes so fast before.

In the afternoon, the Burnell children went home. There were visitors. Isabel and Lottie liked visitors, so they ran upstairs to change their clothes. But Kezia quietly went out of the back of the house. There was nobody there. She climbed onto the big white gates.

Presently, she saw two small shapes coming along the road towards her. Now she could see that one was in front and one close behind. Now she could see that they were the Kelveys. Kezia jumped down from the gate. She started to run away, but then she changed her mind. She stopped and waited. The Kelveys came nearer, and beside them walked their shadows, very long. Kezia climbed back onto the gate. The Kelveys were coming nearer.

'Hello,' she said as they passed her.

They were so surprised that they stopped walking. Lil gave her silly smile. Else stared.

'You can come and see our doll's house if you want to,' said Kezia.

But Lil's face turned red and she shook her head quickly.

'Why not?' asked Kezia.

Lil opened her mouth. At first, she said nothing, then she said, 'Your mother told our mother that you mustn't speak to us.'

'Oh, well,' said Kezia. She didn't know what to say. 'It doesn't

34

'You can come and see our doll's house if you want to,' said Kezia

matter. You can come and see our doll's house all the same. Come on. Nobody's looking.'

But Lil shook her head still harder.

'Don't you want to?' asked Kezia.

Suddenly, something pulled at Lil's skirt. She turned round. Else was looking at her with big eyes, she was looking worried, she wanted to go with Kezia. For a moment, Lil looked back at Else. But then Else gave her skirt a little pull again. So Lil started forward. Kezia led the way. They followed her, like two little lost cats, to where the doll's house stood.

'There it is,' said Kezia.

There was a pause. Lil breathed very loudly; Else was still as stone.

'I'll open it for you,' said Kezia kindly. She opened the front of the doll's house and they all looked inside.

'There's the living-room and the dining-room, and that's the . . .'

'Kezia!'

It was Aunt Beryl's voice. They turned around. Aunt Beryl stood at the back door, staring as if she could not believe what she saw.

'How dare you invite the little Kelveys to come here!' Aunt Beryl said. Her voice was cold and very angry. 'Kezia, you know very well that you must not talk to them. Run away, children, run away at once. And don't come back again.' And she came out and chased them out as if she were chasing chickens.

'Off you go, immediately!' she called, cold and proud.

She didn't need to tell them more than once. Their faces were burning, red with shame, and they tried to make themselves very small. Lil hurried off, and Else, looking as if she did not quite understand what was happening, followed her.

'You disobedient little girl!' said Aunt Beryl to Kezia. She

'How dare you invite the little Kelveys to come here!' Aunt Beryl said.
Her voice was cold and very angry.

turned and shut up the doll's house quickly and noisily.

Beryl's afternoon had been awful. She had received a very frightening letter from Willie Brent. He wanted to meet her that evening; he wanted to meet her secretly. If she did not appear, he wrote, he would come to the house and ask for her. He would tell her family all about their secret meetings!

But now, after frightening the little Kelvey girls and shouting angrily at Kezia, she suddenly felt much better. Her heart felt lighter. She went back into the house, singing a little song to herself.

After the Kelveys had gone quite a long way from the Burnells' house, they sat down to rest at the side of the road. Lil's cheeks were still burning! She took off her hat and held it on her knee. Silently, they looked across the fields, past the river, to the group of trees where Logan's cows were standing. What were their thoughts?

Presently, Else moved closer to her sister. By now she had forgotten the angry lady. She put out a finger, touched her sister's hat and smiled her rare smile.

'I did see the little lamp,' she said softly.

Then they were both silent once more.

The Garden Party

It was a perfect day for a garden party. The gardener had been working since early in the morning, cutting the grass. The roses looked perfect.

During breakfast, the men came to put up the marquee.

'Where do you want them to put the marquee, mother?'

'My dear child, don't ask me. This year, you children must do everything. You'll have to go, Laura.'

Laura went out into the garden, still holding a piece of bread and butter. She loved having to arrange things. But when she saw the men standing there with all their equipment, she felt shy. She wished she was not holding the bread and butter.

'Good morning,' she said, copying her mother's voice. But that sounded wrong and she continued, like a little girl, 'Oh – er – have you come – is it about the marquee?'

'That's right.'

The men were friendly, and Laura felt better. She wanted to say 'What a beautiful morning!' but she must be business-like.

'What about there?' she pointed.

But the men did not agree with her.

'Look here, miss, that's the place. Against those trees. Over there.'

She did not want the marquee to hide the beautiful trees, but the men were already moving off towards the trees. But the men were so nice. She liked them better than the boys she danced with and the boys who came to supper on Sunday night. She took a big bite of bread and butter.

Then someone called from the house, 'Laura, where are you? Telephone, Laura!'

'Coming!' She ran back to the house, across the garden. In the

The men were friendly and Laura felt better. She wanted to say what a beautiful morning it was, but she must be business-like.

hall, her father and brother were getting ready to go to the office.

'I say, Laura,' said her brother, Laurie, speaking very fast, 'could you just look at my coat before this afternoon?'

'I will,' she said. Suddenly, she added. 'Oh, I do love parties, don't you?'

'Yes,' he said in his warm and boyish voice, 'but don't forget the telephone.'

All the doors in the house were open. People ran from room to room, calling to each other. There was a strange sound – they were moving the piano. The front doorbell rang. It was the man from the flower shop. But there were so many beautiful flowers – Laura could not believe it.

'There must be some mistake!'

Her mother suddenly appeared. 'It's quite right. I ordered them. Aren't they lovely!'

They tried out the piano. Laura's sister sang. Then a servant came in and asked about the sandwiches. There were fifteen different kinds of sandwiches. Then a man came to deliver some cream cakes from the baker's shop.

'Bring them in and put them on the table,' ordered the cook.

Laura and her sister tried some of the cream cakes. Then Laura suggested, 'Let's go into the garden, out by the back way.'

But they could not get through the back door. The cook and Sadie were there talking to the baker's man.

Something had happened.

Their faces were worried. The baker's man was telling them something.

'What's the matter? What's happened?'

'There's been a horrible accident,' said the cook. 'A man killed.'

'Killed! Where? How? When?'

'Do you know those little houses just below here, miss?'

'Well, there's a young man called Scott. His horse ran away and he was killed.'

Of course she knew them.

'Well, there's a young man living there, called Scott. He's a driver. His horse ran away at the corner of Hawke Street this morning, and he was thrown out onto the back of his head. He was killed.'

'Dead!' Laura stared at the man.

'Dead when they picked him up,' said the man. 'They were taking his body home as I came here.' He turned to the cook and added, 'He's left a wife and five little children.'

'How are we going to stop everything?' she asked her sister, José.

'Stop everything, Laura?' José cried. 'What do you mean?'

'Stop the garden party, of course.'

But José was surprised. 'Stop the garden party? My dear Laura, don't be so silly. Of course we can't stop the garden party.'

'But we can't possibly have a garden party with a man dead just outside the front gate.'

The houses where the dead man had lived were not exactly outside the front gate. Still, they were too near the house. They were ugly and poor. In their small gardens, there was nothing but a few weak vegetables, sick chickens, and old tomato tins. Children ran everywhere. When the Sheridan children were little, they were not allowed to go near those houses. They might catch some illness or learn some bad language from the children who lived there. Now that they were grown up, Laura and her sisters sometimes walked past the little houses. They found them horrible, but still they went, because they wanted to see everything.

'But the band. Just think what the band would sound like to that poor woman,' said Laura.

'Oh, Laura,' said José angrily. 'You can't stop a band playing every time someone has an accident. I'm sorry that the accident happened, too. I feel just as sorry as you do. But you won't bring that man back to life by feeling sad about it.'

'Well, I'm going straight up to tell mother.'

'Do, dear,' said José.

♦

'Mother, can I come into your room?' Laura asked.

'Of course, child. Why, what's the matter?' Mrs Sheridan turned round. She was trying on a new hat.

'Mother, a man was killed this morning . . .' Laura began to say.

'Not in the garden?' her mother asked.

'No, no!'

'Oh, how you frightened me!' Mrs Sheridan took off the big hat.

'But listen, Mother,' said Laura. She told the terrible story. 'Of course, we can't have our party, can we?' she asked. 'They will hear the band and everybody arriving. They'll hear us, Mother, they're nearly neighbours!'

To Laura's surprise, her mother behaved just like José. She even seemed to be amused. She refused to take Laura seriously.

'But my dear child, you must be sensible. We heard about it by accident. When someone dies there in the usual way, we don't know about it. Then we would still have our party, wouldn't we?'

'Mother, aren't we being heartless?' she asked.

'My dear child!' Mrs Sheridan got up and came over to Laura, carrying the hat. Before Laura could stop her, she put the hat on Laura's head. 'The hat is yours. It's much too young for me. You look lovely. Look at yourself!'

'But Mother . . .' Laura began to say. She couldn't look at herself. She turned away from the mirror.

Mrs Sheridan was impatient. 'You are being very silly, Laura,' she said coldly. 'People like that don't want us to give up our parties. You're just spoiling everybody's enjoyment.'

'I don't understand,' said Laura. She walked quickly out of the room and into her own bedroom. There, the first thing she saw was a lovely girl in the mirror, in a big black hat with gold flowers. She could not believe it. She had never looked like that before. 'Is mother right?' she thought. And now, she hoped her mother was right. For a moment, she thought again about the poor woman in the little house with the five children. She thought about people carrying the dead man's body into the house. But now it seemed less real. It was like a picture in a newspaper. I'll remember it again after the party's over, she decided.

By half-past two, everything was ready for the party to begin.

The band had arrived. Then Laurie arrived and hurried away to change his clothes. Laura remembered the accident and wanted to tell him about it.

'Laurie!'

'Hello.' Laurie turned round and saw Laura in her new hat. His eyes grew big. 'Laura! You look wonderful!' said Laurie. 'What an absolutely beautiful hat!'

'Is it?' Laura said quietly. She smiled at Laurie and didn't tell him about the accident after all.

Soon after, the guests started to arrive. The band started to play, and waiters ran from the house to the marquee. There were people everywhere: walking around the garden, talking, looking at the flowers, moving on across the grass. They were like bright birds. Everyone was happy. They smiled into each other's eyes.

'Laura, how well you look!'

'Laura, what a lovely hat!'

'Laura, I've never seen you look so wonderful!'

And Laura answered softly, 'Have you had tea? Won't you have an ice?'

And the perfect afternoon slowly passed.

Laura helped her mother with the goodbyes. They stood side by side until it was all over.

'All over,' said Mrs Sheridan. 'Find the others, Laura. Let's go and have some coffee. I'm so tired.'

They all went out to the empty marquee.

Mr Sheridan ate a sandwich. He took another. 'I suppose you didn't hear about an awful accident that happened today?' he said.

'My dear,' said Mrs Sheridan, 'we did. Laura wanted to stop the party.'

'Oh Mother!' Laura did not want anybody to laugh at her.

'All the same, it was a terrible thing,' said Mr Sheridan. 'The

There were people everywhere: walking around the garden, talking, looking at the flowers, moving on across the grass.

man was married too. He lived just below here, and he leaves a wife and children, they say.'

Everyone was silent. Mrs Sheridan wished her husband hadn't talked about the accident. Suddenly she saw all the food left on the table. She had an idea.

'I know,' she said. 'Let's make up a basket. Let's send some of this food to that poor woman. The children will love it. Don't you agree? The woman's sure to have people coming to the house. And it's all ready!' She jumped up. 'Laura! Get me that big basket!'

'But Mother, do you really think it's a good idea?' said Laura.

It was strange that once again, Laura was different from the others. Would the poor woman really want the food left over from their party?

'Of course,' said her mother. 'What's the matter with you today?'

Laura ran for the basket. Her mother filled it with food.

'Take it yourself, Laura dear,' she said. 'Don't change your clothes. No, wait, take these flowers too. Poor people like flowers.'

'The flowers are wet. They'll spoil Laura's dress,' José said.

'Only the basket then. Run along,' said her mother.

It was growing dark as Laura shut the garden gates. The little houses down below were in deep shadow. How quiet it seemed after the afternoon. She was still too full of the party to realize that she was going to visit the home of a dead man.

She crossed the broad road, and entered the dark, smoky little street. Women hurried past and men stood around. Children played outside the doors. There were weak lights inside the houses and shadows moved across the windows. Laura hurried on. She wished that she had put a coat on. Her dress shone, and her hat with the gold flowers seemed to be too big. People must be staring at her. It was a mistake to come. Should she go back home?

47

No, it was too late. This was the house. There was a dark little group of people standing outside. A woman, very old, sat on a chair next to the gate, with her feet on a newspaper. The voices stopped as Laura drew near. The group separated, as if they were waiting for Laura.

Laura was terribly nervous. 'Is this Mrs Scott's house?' she asked a woman.

The woman smiled strangely. 'It is.'

Laura wanted to go away. But she walked up the narrow path and knocked on the door. She felt the people silently staring at her. I'll just leave the basket and go, she decided. I won't wait for them to take all the things out of the basket.

Then the door opened. A little woman in black appeared.

Laura said, 'Are you Mrs Scott?'

But the woman only answered, 'Walk in, please, miss,' and closed the door behind Laura.

'No,' said Laura, 'I don't want to come in. I only want to leave this basket. Mother sent –'

The little woman did not seem to hear her. 'This way, please, miss,' she said, and Laura followed her.

Laura found herself in the poor low little kitchen. The room was smoky and dark. There was a woman sitting in front of the fire.

'Em,' said the little woman who had let her in. 'Em! It's a young lady.' She turned to Laura. She said. 'I'm her sister, miss. You'll excuse her, won't you?'

'Oh, but of course!' said Laura. 'Please, please don't worry her. I – I only want to leave . . .'

But the woman in front of the fire turned round. She had been crying and her face looked terrible. She did not seem to understand why Laura was there. What did it mean? Why was this stranger standing in the kitchen with a basket? What was it all about? The poor woman began to cry again.

The woman sitting in front of the fire turned round. She had been crying and her face looked terrible.

'It's all right, my dear,' said the other woman. 'I'll thank the young lady.'

Again she began to say, 'You'll excuse her, miss, I'm sure,' and she tried to smile.

Laura only wanted to get out, to get away. She left the room. A door opened and she walked straight through into the bedroom, where the dead man was lying.

'You'd like to look at him, wouldn't you?' said Em's sister, and she went past Laura to the bed. 'Don't be afraid, miss,' she said, and she pulled down the cover. 'He looks like a picture. There's nothing to show where he was hurt. Come along, my dear.'

Laura came.

There lay a young man, fast asleep – sleeping so deeply that he was far, far away from them both. So far away, so peaceful. He was dreaming. Never wake him up again. His head lay on the soft pillow, his eyes were closed; they were blind under the closed eyelids. He was deep in his dream. What did garden parties and baskets and beautiful clothes matter to him? He was far from all those things. He was wonderful, beautiful. While they were laughing and while the band was playing, this wonderful thing was happening here. Happy... happy... 'All is well,' said that sleeping face. 'I am happy.'

But all the same you had to cry, and Laura couldn't go out of the room without saying something to him. Laura was crying loudly, like a child.

'Forgive my hat,' she said.

And this time she did not wait for Em's sister. She found her own way out of the door, down the path past all those people. At the corner of the street, she met Laurie.

Laurie appeared out of the shadows. 'Is that you, Laura?'

'Yes.'

'Mother was getting worried. Was it all right?'

'Yes. Oh Laurie!' she took his arm, and pressed against him.

'I say, you're not crying, are you?' asked her brother.

Laura shook her head. She was crying.

Laurie put his arm round her shoulder. 'Don't cry,' he said in his warm, loving voice. 'Was it awful?'

'No,' said Laura, still crying. 'It was wonderful. But Laurie —' She stopped, she looked at her brother. 'Isn't life,' she tried to say, 'isn't life —' But she couldn't explain what life was. It did not matter. Laurie understood perfectly.

'*Isn't* it, dear?' said Laurie.

ACTIVITIES

Bliss, pages 1–6

Before you read

1 Look at the Word List at the back of the book. Check words in your dictionary if necessary. Then find:

    a three words for things you can eat.

    b the name of an animal.

    c two things that children play with.

    d two parts of a human face.

    e a word to describe a person with a high opinion of him/herself.

    f a word that means a very pleasant feeling, and another word that is an unpleasant feeling. ·

2 Read the Introduction to the book. Make sentences by joining these names on the left to words on the right.

    a Harry   enters a different world.

    b Reginald   receives a doll's house.

    c The Burnell family   has the perfect family.

    d Laura   has a low opinion of his wife.

3 Are these sentences right or wrong?

    a Mansfield's first marriage lasted one day.

    b Her friends thought she was very funny and clever.

    c Winters in southern Europe were too cold for her.

    d She wrote plays as well as short stories.

    e She earned a lot of money from her writing.

4 The first story in this book is called 'Bliss'. Bliss is a feeling of complete happiness. The woman in the picture on page 5 feels blissful. Do you ever feel like this? What would make you feel like this? Talk to other students.

5 Tick (✓) the things which are true about Bertha on pages 1–6.

   a ..... She often forgets her house key.

   b ..... Colour is important to her.

   c ..... She spends most of the day with her baby.

   d ..... She has known Miss Fulton a long time.

   e ..... Cats make her feel uncomfortable.

After you read

6 Complete these sentences.

   a We know Bertha is rich because …

   b Nurse is pleased when there is a phone call for Bertha because …

   c Miss Fulton is a mystery because …

   d Harry says he doesn't like Miss Fulton because …

Bliss, pages 6–13

Before you read

7 Bertha's life is too perfect. Is something going to happen to spoil her 'bliss'? What could it be? Think of three different ideas. Compare ideas with another student.

8 A black cat follows a grey cat across Bertha's garden. She has 'a strange, cold feeling' when she sees them. Why, do you think?

While you read

9 Complete the sentences with the names of people at Bertha's table.

   a .... wears green and white and looks like a pear tree.

   b .... wears yellow and looks like a monkey.

   c .... looks pale like the moon.

   d .... is going to open a theatre.

   e .... arrives late and enjoys the food.

   f .... wears a dress like the moon.

After you read

10 Work in pairs. The guests have gone. Bertha and Harry are alone. Have their conversation.

Student A: You are Bertha. You say, 'Oh, what is going to happen now?'

Student B: You are Harry. You don't know that Bertha saw you with Miss Fulton in the hall. You say, 'What do you mean, my dear?'

Mr Reginald Peacock's Day, pages 15–19

Before you read

11 Look at the picture on page 18. Who is happy in this family and who isn't? Why might this be? Write some ideas.

While you read

12 Reginald's views are not the same as the truth! Underline the best words in *italics*.

  a Reginald's wife wakes him up *rudely / quietly* each morning.

  b Reginald *is / isn't* vain.

  c Reginald's wife *is happy to / doesn't want to* cook bacon for him each morning.

  d *Reginald has argued with all the servants. / His wife can't find the right kind of servant*.

  e He thinks only about *his own / his wife's* feelings.

After you read

13 Think of two adjectives to describe Reginald and his wife. Use a dictionary if you like. Compare your choices with another student. Are they the same?

Mr Reginald Peacock's Day, pages 20–26

Before you read

14 Look at the letter from Aenone Fell on page 18. Reginald's pupils do not share his wife's opinion of him. Why is this, do you think? Discuss this with other students.

15 Mr Peacock loves giving advice. Read what he says – who is each piece of advice for?

   a 'Sing as if you were in love.' ....

   b 'Sit down and let me sing to you.' ....

   c 'Think about the flowers while you sing.' ....

   d 'Do not be afraid. Let yourself go.' ....

   e 'Smell these flowers and listen.' ....

   f 'Practise in front of a mirror.' ....

After you read

16 Answer these questions.

   a A 'peacock' is a bird with a very large and beautiful tail of blue and green, which it shows off to female birds. Why is it a good surname for Reginald?

   b 'I'm going out to dinner,' says Reginald.
      'But why didn't you tell me before?' asks his wife.
      Reginald thinks his wife's question is rude. Do you agree with him?

   c Reginald says to his wife, 'Dear lady, I should be so charmed!' Why are these words so wrong?

The Doll's House, pages 27–32

Before you read

17 The children in this story receive a wonderful doll's house as a gift. What was the most exciting gift you received as a child? Tell another student about it.

While you read

18 Are these sentences right (✓) or wrong (✗)?

   a The doll's house is too big to bring into the house. .....

   b The house makes the girls feel sad. .....

   c The girls hurry to school the next morning because they are late. .....

   d All the girls at school want to be Isabel's friend. .....

e The rich parents do not want their children to talk to
the Kelveys.   .....

f The Kelveys wear clothes made from other people's
table covers and curtains.   .....

g The girls all eat the same for lunch.   .....

After you read

19 Answer these questions.

    a Why don't the dolls look as if they belong in the doll's house?

    b Why can't the girls from school stay to tea or come into the house?

    c Why are Mr and Mrs Burnell unhappy about the school that their daughters go to?

    d Why does the teacher have a special voice for the Kelveys?

    e Why doesn't Else speak or smile?

The Doll's House, pages 33–38

Before you read

20 Which of these things will happen, do you think?

    a The Kelveys will see the doll's house.

    b The Kelveys won't see the doll's house.

    c Something terrible will happen to the Kelveys.

While you read

21 Use these words to complete the sentences.

angry better bored chases invites nasty prison
secretly wonderful worried

    a The girls at school are .... with the doll's house.

    b They decide to be .... to the Kelveys instead.

    c Lena gets .... because the other girls laugh at her.

    d Lena says to the Kelveys that their father is in ....

    e The other girls think this is ....

    f Kezia .... Lil and Else to see the doll's house.

g Aunt Beryl .... the little Kelveys out of the gate.

h Aunt Beryl has been seeing Willie Brent ....

i She's .... that her family will find out.

j She feels .... after she's nasty to the Kelveys.

After you read

22 When the Kelveys get home from school, they tell their mother about Kezia and the doll's house. Work with two other students. Have their conversation.

Student A: You are Lil Kelvey. Start like this: *On the way home from school today …*

Student B: You are Else Kelvey. Tell your mother what you saw and how you felt.

Student C: You are Mrs Kelvey. Ask lots of questions.

The Garden Party, pages 39–44

Before you read

23 Work in pairs. You are planning a garden party for next weekend. Decide on your plans for: the place, food and drink, guests, entertainment. Then tell another pair about your party.

While you read

24 Write the names. Who:

a decides where to put the marquee?   ....

b goes to the office?   .... and ....

c orders all the flowers?   ....

d brings bad news?   ....

e is dead?   ....

f wants to stop the garden party?   ....

g doesn't think the neighbours will be
upset by the party?   ....

h changes her mind when she sees herself
in the mirror?   ....

25 Work with two other students. The baker's man brings the news about Mr Scott's death. Have this conversation.

Student A: You are the baker's man. Tell the others the news.

Student B: You are Sadie. You are very upset by the news. You know the family well.

Student C: You are the cook. You want to hear all the details.

The Garden Party, pages 45–51

Before you read

26 The Sheridans are not changing their plans for a party. Think of reasons for them to stop the party. Think of reasons for them to continue the party. Write two lists. Show your ideas to other students.

While you read

27 Underline the best way to complete these sentences.

    a Laura decides not to tell Laurie about the accident because ...
- it will spoil his mood • she doesn't think it's important
- he likes her hat

    b The party goes ...
- well • quickly • badly

    c Mrs Sheridan ... about the accident.
- is sorry • doesn't want to hear • wants to talk

    d Mrs Sheridan sends Laura to Mrs Scott ...
- with a basket of food • with food and flowers
- to say sorry

    e When Laura gets into the dark little street, she feels ...
- uncomfortable • pleased • cold

    f Mrs Scott ...
- is pleased to see Laura • doesn't know what Laura wants
- doesn't want the basket

    g Laura ... see the dead body.
- doesn't • isn't expecting to • is afraid to

After you read

28 Answer these questions.

    a Why does Laura say 'Forgive my hat,' to the dead man, do you think?

    b Do you think Laura has seen a dead body before?

    c Can you finish Laura's sentence: 'Isn't life …?' What does she want to say, do you think?

29 Talk to other students. In what ways are Kezia in 'The Doll's House' and Laura in 'The Garden Party' similar? Do you think the writer likes them?

Writing

30 Choose one of the four stories. Write what happens to the main character(s) immediately after the story finishes.

31 Before she discovers that her husband and Miss Fulton are lovers, Bertha has a happy life. She doesn't have much responsibility, though. Write her diary for an ordinary day.

32 Reginald Peacock's wife writes to her sister. She tells her about Reginald's behaviour. Give Reginald's wife a name and write her letter.

33 In 'The Doll's House', the girls at school are cruel to the Kelveys because they are poor. What do you think the Kelveys should do? Why are children in groups cruel to other children? What can we do to protect children from this kind of treatment? Write your opinions.

34 Laura leaves the dead man's house and goes home. Two of the dead man's relatives talk about her visit. What do they think of her? Write their conversation.

35 Choose one of these pairs of characters. Describe and compare them. Say what the writer thinks of them. Say what you think of them.

    a Bertha Young and Miss Fulton

    b Reginald Peacock and his wife

    c Aunt Beryl and Kezia

    d Laura and her mother

36 Write a description of a garden party, a dinner party or a birthday party that you have been to. Where was it? Who came? What did everyone wear? What food and drink was there? What did people talk about?

37 The Burnell girls are very excited about the wonderful doll's house. Think of the first time that you saw something or somewhere wonderful. Describe what it was like and how you felt.

38 Think of a short story writer in your language. Find out about his/her life and work and what people think of them. Write a short piece about this writer.

39 Think of an idea for a short story. It can describe one important moment in a person's life. Perhaps the person discovers something, or something unexpected happens. Write a plan, then write the story.

Answers for the Activities in this book are available from the Penguin Readers website. A free Activity Worksheet is also available from the website. Activity Worksheets are part of the Penguin Teacher Support Programme, which also includes Progress Tests and Graded Reader Guidelines. For more information, please visit:
www.penguinreaders.com.

WORD LIST

bacon (n) meat from a pig that is salty and cut into thin pieces

band (n) a group of musicians who play together

bliss (n) complete happiness

charm (v) to make people like you by behaving in an attractive way

cheek (n) the soft round part of your face below your eye

Countess (n) a title of a woman with a very high social position

delightful (adj) very pleasing

disobedient (adj) refusing to obey

doll (n) a toy that looks like a person, especially a baby

eyelid (n) a piece of skin that covers your eye when you close it

for instance for example

grape (n) a small green or dark red fruit that grows in bunches

jug (n) an open container with a handle for pouring liquids

marquee (n) a large tent used for an outdoor event or a party

monkey (n) a small brown animal with a long tail that climbs trees

neighbourhood (n) an area of a town and the people who live there

nod (v) to move your head up and down to mean 'yes' or to show understanding

obvious (adj) very clear and easy to notice or understand

only too (adv) very

pear (n) a green or yellow fruit, round at the bottom and thinner at the top

presently (adv) after a short time; soon

rope (n) a piece of strong thick string

shame (n) the unpleasant feeling when you know you have done something bad, and people think badly of you

skip (v) to jump over a rope that moves under your feet and over your head

sleeve (n) the part of something you wear that covers your arm

stiff (adj) difficult to bend or move

stockings (n) very thin clothes that women wear over their feet and legs

swallow (v) to make food or drink go down your throat

tiny (adj) very small

vain (adj) too proud of your appearance